Random Thoughts

Monita Sharpe

BookLeaf Publishing

India | USA | UK

Presentation by *BookLeaf Publishing*

Web: www.bookleafpub.com

E-mail: info@bookleafpub.com

ISBN: 978-93-5744-961-8

First edition 2022

DEDICATION

To my family. I love you! Thanks for sharing
me with all who walk in our circle. My life is
complete because you are in it. James (IV).
Epiphany. James (V). Merit. Shekinah.
Cataleya, mi nieta.

ACKNOWLEDGEMENT

God. Thank You for the ability to think and create. James C. Sharpe, IV, freeing me to write. Jacqueline D. Navarrete and T. Ford for competing with me. Epiphany Sharpe. James C. Sharpe, V. Merit V. Sharpe. Shekinah A. Sharpe for giving me content and sharing me with so many. Cataleya M.N. Jones, for making me an Abuelita.

PREFACE

Random thoughts roam my mind daily. Some take residence until they are processed. Some remain in residence after being processed. These poems depict roamings that found a way to the page. Connect to the ones that intrigue you. Dismiss the others as random thoughts.

She Went Without Me

I thought we had a thing
I guess it was a fling
She went without me

I am accustomed to routine
I always knew what to bring
But, she went without me

Our paths diverged
But, I thought we still converged
On the thing with which we had history

I was going off the norm
Little knowing she had moved on
Which is why she went without me

I held on to the past
I should have known it wouldn't last
But it all happened way too fast
She went without me

Life throws you lots of blows

You have to count your woes
But don't make friends your foes
Because they go without you

We must learn to move on
For our past is often gone
We have memories on which to hold on
When they go without us

No love need be lost
Even if your feelings are tossed
Because she went without you

What was – was just that – "was"
It made life during that season a "buzz"
But now she goes without me

I thought we had a thing
We did! It wasn't a fling
She just now has to go on without me.

Family

Family
We don't choose them
We inherit them like we inherit freckles
one at at time,
sometimes in a cluster,
often they just appear with no warning
They come to us automatically

God sends them our way
to stick and stay
and we have to figure out
how to live with them,
how to love them
and hopefully how to like them

Family
We don't choose them
They don't choose us
We get them like we get the flu,
or a cold,
or the mumps
or a bruise
But in growing up, in and around and with them
we can learn so much
And if we learn well

We live well

We learn to deal with and put up with
shenanigans and malarkey
We learn to tolerate and celebrate
We see inside others –
the good, the great,
the dismal, the decaying
the reality of life
of life with loved ones

Family
We don't choose them
We grow up with them like we grow up with
books
       or with television
       or cars - old, new, used, run-down
       or bicycles
We hear them
We see them
We laugh with them
We laugh at them

Family refines our character
Family shapes our morality
(which may be reshaped later)
Family inoculates us to systems
     and processes
     of who, how, what…

Family
We don't choose them
Yet, we love them like we love ice cream
       or candy
       or popcorn
       or chicken
We honor them
We support them
We celebrate them

Family
We don't choose them
We are them

My Eye

Really! A black eye!
I am 53 and I get a black eye

You sucker punch me
Unawares, in the dark, when I am caught off
guard

You have not enough girth nor boldness
To even let me see you swing

But, the sting…
And sting it does

The swelling
Swell it does

My right eyebrow is now adorned with the bump
The size of a walnut
Yet, I am not a walnut tree

Then ice aches it
But I am fortunate
No headache ensues

But now we get the dark colors of the color
wheel
Badly applied make-up to the right eye only
Smeared mascara

From a fine line to a deep green
Deep green to purple
Purple to blue black

Inquisitive eyes
Inquisitive stares
Inquisitive…questions come

What do I say?
Do I lie?
Do I tell the truth?
What do I say?

Emergency Room visit late Saturday Night
ER doctor saying, "hmmmmm, let's see"

Dark dreary, dreadful
Stiff-armed in the eye

Payback is something

You rear up and strike
You hit me, I hit back

I get the best of you
You can bring me no more harm

You have been replaced

But thank you for showing me my resilience
Thank you for showing me I heal quickly
Thank you for showing me patience (as I heal)

And to think, you are a bedroom bench
A piece of furniture
A matching settee to a sleigh bed

You should have stayed on all fours
You hit me
You lose your place
Lesson learned

Hidden in plain view

Hidden in plain view
Or so I think
Doing all the things I know not to do
Does that make me a fake or a fink
  Since I lie to myself and think I lie to you
Yet, I hide in plain view

I know but I just can't do
I so want to please me or is it you
Who I want to please and appease
As I hide in plain view?

Wait, if I am hidden in plain view
(or so I think)
    and you see me then I'm not hiding at
all
    so when I wink and blink
    you smile and nod because you know
    I am hidden in plain view

The Runner

I compromise because it is so hard to rise
        Above the odds and against the grain
Your expectations are high but are they high
or am I reaching too low because
I refuse to fight to rise?

Life is a challenge
Challenges are a challenge
        When faced with challenges
        I run, falter, fade, hide, assimilate,
acclimate
Because I refuse to fight to rise

Fighting is hard. You trained me as a runner
        Not a boxer
so running is easy for me
I forgot that we run against competition
not from them…

Parents

Parents.
    Our first gods. guides. teachers.
Parents.
    Our first security. safety. trust.
Parents.
    Our first love. laughs. temples.

Then we grow.

Do parents then forget?
    Or don't they know
    that we still need them?

Their nurture. wisdom. guidance.

Weeds

Plants grow with care,
       love, nurture
Need watering, light,
       sometimes dark
Must weed 'em, eradicate dead,
       talk to 'em
Plants flourish with care
Plants by definition – need outsiders
       outside support, another

Weeds grow
       weeds need no care, little light
       water

They can grow in too much hot
       too much cold
       too little light
       too much light
       too little dark
       too much dark
Weeds need no time, no attention,
       no training, no care
Weeds will grow with you,
       without you
       in spite of you even

Children…plants
> yet they often grow as weeds

Your fear

Your fear causes you to fight and take flight
Your fear causes you to lie and manipulate
Your fear causes you to be unjust
If indeed you are superior – put us on the same
playing field and you will win
　But you won't
You are not superior and your fear even
indicates inferior and inferiority

A Poet?

What makes a poet a poet?
Someone classifying her as so?
Writing in less conventional ways?
Saying something but not plainly?
Making others work to figure out what was said
'cuz words used differed from words meant?

Hmmmm…

Is it the bearing/bare-ing of the soul?
Is it the bravery to say a thing without saying it?
Hmmmm…
What makes a poet a poet?

The Boomer, Gen X, Millennial

As Boomer, I still stand the victor at Hopscotch
Hopscotch with friends on the faded, cemented
Hopscotch boards at the nearby elementary
school.

The board crafted to teach counting by 10s,
  (so I win at 120).
Gen X gets stuck on 70.
Millennial can't get past 40.

Childhood revisited
Memories relived
Experiences re-explored
Adventures re-invented

Hopscotch…
so simple
  BUT
so telling…
coordination, skill, vitality,
balance, youth, hand-eye coordination,
memory, hopping, one-leg balance,

both legs bending, stooping, tossing,

Boomer still stands the victor at Hopscotch.

She Can't Leave

She can't leave
What is that?
She knows better
But then we don't always do what we know,

The mother elephant fights for her cub
Nothing can harm it – not even dad
So how can the mother elephant put her cub in
harms' way?
How can she be concerned about her place in the
herd
So much so that she neglects her place in her
home
She can't leave.

How does she beg and plead to be in the game,
Get in – then refuse to bat
She does not swing because sometimes she
strikes out.

All hitters strike out.
Every one.
Doesn't matter how good hitters hit,
At some point a pitcher strikes out every hitter

But hitters still go up to bat
Hitters still swing
Hitters still give it their all.
Hitters don't run away from the game because of
a hitting slump.

How does she beg and plead for ice cream,
finally get it, and let it melt.
Why ask for it?
Why get it?
Ice cream is vulnerable.
It cannot last on its own.
It has to be frozen or consumed
(or like the wicked witch of the East it melts).
It is wrong, unfair, unjust, and wasteful to ask
for ice cream,
Beg and plead for ice cream and then let it melt.

She can't leave.
She has to protect her cub.
She can't run from the game.
She can't let ice cream melt.

Really? Yes

You get to the point where you ask,
      Really?
      Yes, is the response.

You plan. You prep. You postulate.
You ponder. You perceive. You perspirate.
Yet, you minimize what you see
For what you see is not what you wanted it to
be,
But it is, so…
Really?? You ask.
Then, Yes!

You study. You sow. You speculate.
You suspend. You surprise. You suspect.
Yet, what is in front of you is NOT what you
hoped.
What you currently have is not what you sought
Yet, things are what they are
Thus, "Really?" You ask.
Yes, is the response.

You energize. You enthuse. You expect.
You encourage. You examine. You exhort.
But the outcome looks like mashed potatoes

Bet you hoped for baked potatoes
Meanwhile mashed potatoes are your lot
       Really?
       Yes, Mashed potatoes are sumptuous,
you are told.

You achieve. You aspire. You accelerate.
You acclaim. You afford. You anticipate.
This time your lemons are lemonade –
all natural no sugar – good for you – not good to
you.
Really?? Really? After all I've done, you ask.
Yes! Was the stare back at you - point blank.

You consider. You cancel. You contemplate.
You carouse. You contend. You concentrate.
You decide that though your lot is somewhat
vacant, it is a lot nonetheless –
thus, you acclaim
Really!
Yes!! You respond, now you can't wait.

Essence of Writing

What is the essence of writing? Of writing
poetry
Is it to pass something along?
Or alone?
To express.
To expose.
Is it to rid yourself of looming emotions
           through thoughts on a page
that scream like the toddler who can't get his
way
or like the infant whose cries for milk, due to
hunger, exasperating mom.

Is written expression a craft?
An art.
A skill.
Or is written expression- literally-written
expression?

Who judges this as good?
Others who read it?
See it?
Learn it?
Need it?
Others who study it?

When you, the one who penned it,
simply need to expose it
because like your bladder,
when full,
it has to come out
or you will explode.

It. It. It.
What is the it we talk about?
The it that has no name.
The it we are taught to name as representative of
what was,
or what is,
or what is to come.

Then, do we notice it?
read it?
uncover it?
Do we disclose it?
isolate it?
Separate it?
Do we reveal it?
Or simply write it, knowing that it will not make
itself known
(like the inner city kid who struggles at no fault
of his own,
has talent and now is known and grown and
soon gone).

Written expression.
Who judges?
Who is qualified to judge?
You?
Anyone?

I ask again, in case you missed the question the
first time…
What is the essence of writing?

Smorgasbord

There is a smorgasbord in front of you
You leave it for fast food
Now fast food satisfies not
You desire the smorgasbord

Choices

Clank goes the jail cell bars again
Just when I thought I was at the end of this rope
called probation
You yank it hard to show me who's in charge
    because your purpose in life belittles those
    whose Choice belittled them already

Roses with thorns fighting for their beauty to be
evident
  yet with traces of fight and frustration
Caterpillar's aching to fly, but stuck in the
cocoon of life's poor choices
Sunflowers bearing no seeds yet their purpose of
spreading beauty
    while facing the sun evident

My choices don't make me less than you
My choices gave you something – a job – to do
Your job is not to belittle nor ridicule me
Your job holds me accountable, so I can walk
away free

"Free" that's funny, because free costs a lot
Free is one of the most expensive things I've
bought

and you think because you have a title my
"free" is linked to you
My "free" is only linked to what you do

My choices don't define who I am
My choices simply write a letter of a stance I
took,
  a decision I made, an action transpired

My choices help define me
   yet also refine me
   sometimes even bind me -
     bind me to society
     to status quo
     to those who don't know any better,
     any differently, or how to rise above their
choices.

My choices say what I said and did,
   but they shout what I say and do
Yet do you look at the past me and leave me
bondage to him
   or do you look at the present me and see the
new growth?

Clank! Really?

How did I get here again?

My choices set me free
   but you want my choice to bind me.

My Heart

My heart is torn like a piece of paper,
My eyes are set like a taxidermist's project.
Beating! Beating fast. Breathing, breathing
loudly.
How do I say or what do I say to you?

You left me like a ball on a playground.
Used. Abused. Fun while it lasted but then
    moved on to the next best thing.

My heart beats so loudly,
    I hear it like one hears the drum in a marching
band
My eyes shed tears as if they were raindrops
    on a windshield on a stormy day

For you have moved on.
    You have decided that what you think you
merit - you merit
Discarded am I like the candy wrapper during
Halloween.
    Halloween that I don't celebrate. Halloween
that you believe not in.

My heart aches, aches like feet after running a
marathon.

My eyes burn as if it were allergy season and I
have no allergy meds.

For you.
For you my heart beats.
For you my eyes weep.
For you chase the wind that can't be caught
and we watch you we watch you
we watch you
but not warn you…

For you
For you my heart bleeds
For you my eyes swell
For you run like a child in the streets after her
kite
and we watch you we watch you
we watch you
but don't yell that here comes the car…

Pain Gain

What do we gain from pain?
  an awareness or a hole?
Does our soul deepen or grow shallow?

When tears fall constantly
  or even sporadically
  Does it matter?

Pain is like an umbrella that shields us from joy,
peace, happiness.
They drop down like dew,
  but like dew: joy, peace, happiness disappear
  like dew you never knew they were there
  like dew you never know they left an
impression

Pain shapes us or dishevels us
Pain helps us or hurts us pain
Pain enlightens us or depresses us
  but pain definitely molds us

Do we grow from pain like Joseph?
Do we pine away from pain like Saul?

What do we gain from pain?

Sister Friends

Proverbs says there's a friend that sticks closer
than a brother
(Brother can mean sister)
Friends who round you out
Differ from you
Show you a different path, plan, pursuit

Friends who are candid, courageous, caring
Who emanate from a different background
Who may be in your life for a reason,
    or a season…
    or a lifetime…

Friends from who you are to gather and gain…
    give and glean…
    grow and glow…

One friend talks incessantly and knows much
about much but is somewhat out of touch
    with life, culture, and society
    who's intellect seems to educate not proliferate
her from the knowledge she expectorates
    whose life speaks somewhat contrariness to
her words;
She is a mixed-match pair of socks.

One friend whose health challenges her, changed
her, caged her even
    causes her to naturally help you because she
has been through, is going through, is going to
    she knows much about the body and spirit
    and nature and the natural
    her learning and life is a lesson for you;
She is compression socks.

One friend who is an old cautious wary soul in a
not so old body
    a walking dichotomy herself between caution
and carefree
    an oxymoron of adventure and apprehension,
    her contradiction of inattentiveness and
into-it-ness
    makes you laugh and wonder if she amazes
herself as much as she amasses confusion,
    strikes bewilderment in you;
She is rundown tennis shoes.

One friend whose pristine ways causes you to
evaluate your own
    lives on the periphery of the group
    is bound and bonded to us (through the sister
friend coordinator)
    reminds us that self-care, "extravagance" and
the "extra"

are normal, natural and healthy
    that regardless of the package, the packaging
matters;
She is silk stockings.

One friend is the foundation.
Her travels through life cause her to land in a
different state and in various countries
    as opposed to leaving friends in places where
she visited,
    she grabbed pieces of them and re-planted
them all in one garden,
    which she waters and tills.
For the most part, each re-plant is self-sufficient,
    they thrive in their together garden
    knowing that the foundation they have is
steady;
    the gardener is the best at what she does;
She is the closet.

And the last friend who is often on the periphery
    wonders why she's in the garden,
    how she got in the garden growing like a wild
weed.
Knowing she stands out,
    knowing she differs,
    knowing her state is seldom visited but when
visited:
    brings humor, joy, pensivity to others;

She is a pair of work boots.

Proverbs says there's a friend that sticks closer
than a brother
(Brother means sister, as well)
Friends who sharpen you like a knife sharpener
Who challenge you like a poker player
Who complete you like the last piece of the
puzzle.

Hustle and Bustle or Why?

The hustle and bustle have ended
  The hype has come and gone
You sit on the futon in your library
  Now with your thoughts all alone

Why did you do what you did?
Why did you work so hard??
You ponder, reflect, remember
Now you let down your guard

"So much to do. So little time."
This phrase rings true still today
You want a better life for them
You want them to learn to play

The childhood you had is no longer
The child in you still roams
You want children to share childhood wonders
You want children's "happy" to not groan

Parents rip pleasure from children
Parents' focus is wrong

You the kid, should not perish
You, the kid, should enjoy home

The hustle and bustle has ended
The hype dissipated, is no more
You regret the memories not made
You know the ship left the shore

Why did you do what you did?
Why did you work so hard?
You once were a child with experiences
You wanted to do your part.

Family

Family
  a maze
  a jigsaw puzzle
  a kaleidoscope

Family, a pruning ground
   for failure
   for success
   for courage

Families build hope
  tear it down
  build confidence
  strip it right from under you
     (like a chair pulled out as a prank)

Family grows you
   matures you
nurtures you

Families teach you to love
   to hate
   to live for tomorrow
   to dread tomorrow's arrival

Family is where we get our start
  it makes us
  or breaks us
  or shapes us
    (into who we become…
    or from whom we run)

Thank you family
  for better or worse
  I am who I am because of you

It's A Trap

It's a trap.

Or is it your destiny beckoning you answer the
call
    of your life submission
    which has taken you 56 years to engage…
Dibble here. Dabble there.
Preparation has been all over you like frosting
on a smooth moist chocolate layer cake.

Visible. Pleasing. Desirous.
Entreating.
Do you run?
Do you delay?
Do you stray?

It's a trap.

A trap that affects your whole family
    though your foot is the one entangled.
A trap that binds you to a place,
    and a space,
and a time.
A trap that requires your ingenuity and
edgenuity

as you navigate being bound.
But is bound, bound?
Or is bound, liberating.

Liberating you to create, manifest, pioneer.
Initiate. Instigate. Promulgate. Investigate.

When we move towards our destiny
   all the world conspires with us (for us)
   and some even against us!

Ever really thought about a trap?

A trap catches then releases
Catches prey,
Releases prey
  to its next season,
  next purpose,
  next mission,
  next lot.